Fanciful Victorian Initials

1,142 Decorative Letters from "Punch"

Edited by
CAROL BELANGER GRAFTON

Dover Publications Inc., New York

Publisher's Note

Punch, or the London Charivari, the venerable British humor magazine, has from its inception employed decorative initials in its pages. The use of large, embellished letters to open a manuscript or typeset composition has a long history in the West. The Victorians delighted in all manner of book decoration—the more elaborate the better—and their eclectic borrowing from all periods made the graphic styles of previous ages familiar to readers.

For this volume, Carol Belanger Grafton has selected over 1,000 initial letters from the first 73 years of *Punch,* spanning all but the first few years of Victoria's reign and extending to the beginning of World War One. Grafton has chosen the illustrations on the basis of their draftsmanship and visual interest rather than on art-historical grounds. (Dover has previously published an anthology entitled *Great Drawings and Illustrations from "Punch," 1841–1901: 192 Works by Leech, Keene, du Maurier, May and 21 Others,* edited by Stanley Appelbaum and Richard Kelly [1981, 23110-6], which includes a detailed introduction and biographical sketches of many important artists. Interested readers are referred to this volume.)

Naturally, the initials are arranged alphabetically in this collection. Some letters (A and T) are shown in well over 100 forms each. Others, such as K, Q, X and Z, have only a few interpretations, owing to their rarity as initial letters in English. At the end of the book, the "Miscellaneous" designs, similar in spirit to initials, are comprised of entire words or combinations of letters.

The artists at *Punch* used a visual vocabulary rich in literary allusion and historical and topical reference that was readily understood by their educated and devoted audience. In their original contexts, the initials were closely related to the verbal humor they introduced, often punning on a key word in an article; but even without the texts the graphic invention embodied in these designs has a life of its own that will charm and inspire modern illustrators, advertisers and other users of copyright-free art.

In proper Victorian fashion, lettering styles in the initials are quite diverse. Some hark back to such historic calligraphic hands as Anglo-Saxon and Irish uncials, German blackletter and Italian Chancery cursive. Others are imitative of printing types from classic Romans to nineteenth-century grotesques. There are freely drawn capitals and scripts as well, sometimes rendered with seemingly deliberate artlessness to convey a rustic, untutored feeling.

From a design point of view, the integration of the letters and illustrations is perhaps the most interesting aspect of this collection. In some of the cuts, the letters are extrinsic to the drawings. More frequently, the letters are worked into the designs in a variety of ways. There are a number of "historiated" initials, clearly modeled after those in medieval manuscripts, in which figures enclosed in spaces in the letters tell a story. There are initials in which the alphabetic elements are treated architecturally, rendered in three dimensions as part of the illustrations. Human or animal figures in gymnastic postures, their limbs at odd angles forming the letters, are yet another structural type of initial. Inanimate objects shaped like the letters they represent are another graphic device used regularly by *Punch*'s artists, who explored the textural possibilities of feathers, branches, braids, ribbons and rope in the construction of letter forms, in much the same way that Victorian typefounders did. Less fanciful in conception, but still useful in decoration, are the more or less conventional initials with floral ornament that are scattered among the more figurative designs.

The leering, hook-nosed, pointed-chinned face of Mr. Punch, the journal's mascot, appears on almost every other page of this collection, often accompanied by his little dog Toby. He masquerades in many forms, but most typically as a jester.

Political life, both at home and abroad, was (and is) a central theme of *Punch,* and caricatures of public figures and of national types worked into decorative initials abound in this compendium. Other typically British concerns such as sport, military and naval affairs, as well as theater, music, fashion, art, literature and religion were regular subjects in the journal, and initials with images of these fields are well represented. The well-known British love of animals is amply demonstrated by a veritable Noah's Ark of mammals, birds, reptiles, amphibians, fish and even insects.

Roughly half of the cuts in this book have the artist's signatures, usually as monograms. While full identification is beyond the scope of this note, mention should be made of some of the most prominent illustrators. They include Charles Keene (1823–1891) ; Linley Sambourne (1845–1910) ; John Tenniel (1820–1914) ; Richard Doyle (1824–1883) ; John Leech (1817–1864) ; and C. H. Bennett (active 1860s) .

The initials, tailpieces and related decorative elements in *Punch* are not so well remembered as the larger cartoons, but they gave the magazine an additional visual dimension, and some are real achievements in miniature. As R. G. G. Price points out in *A History of Punch* (1957), the drafting of initials gave artists the chance to develop their technique and to try out ideas and styles they would use later in larger, more important compositions. Today's graphic designers will find limitless inspiration in this treasury of authentic Victorian art.

Copyright © 1984 by Dover Publications, Inc.

All rights reserved under Pan American and International Copyright Conventions.

Published in Canada by General Publishing Company, Ltd., 30 Lesmill Road, Don Mills, Toronto, Ontario.

Published in the United Kingdom by Constable and Company, Ltd.

Fanciful Victorian Initials: 1,142 Letters from "Punch" is a new work, first published by Dover Publications, Inc., in 1984. The selection and arrangement of illustrations, from *Punch, or The London Charivari,* Volumes 1–147 (1841–1914), are by Carol Belanger Grafton. The Publisher's Note was prepared specially for this edition.

DOVER *Pictorial Archive* SERIES

Fanciful Victorian Initials: 1,142 Letters from "Punch" belongs to the Dover Pictorial Archive Series. Up to ten illustrations from this book may be reproduced on any one project or in any single publication free and without special permission. Wherever possible please include a credit line indicating the title of this book, author and publisher. Please address the publisher for permission to make more extensive use of illustrations in this book than that authorized above.

The republication of this book in whole is prohibited.

Manufactured in the United States of America
Dover Publications, Inc., 31 East 2nd Street, Mineola, N.Y. 11501

Library of Congress Cataloging in Publication Data
Main entry under title:

Fanciful victorian initials.

(Dover pictorial archive series)
    1. Initials. 2. Decoration and ornament, Victorian. 3. Punch—Illustrations. I. Grafton, Carol Belanger. II. Punch.
NK3625.V53F36   1984   745.6'1   83-20597
ISBN 0-486-24604-3

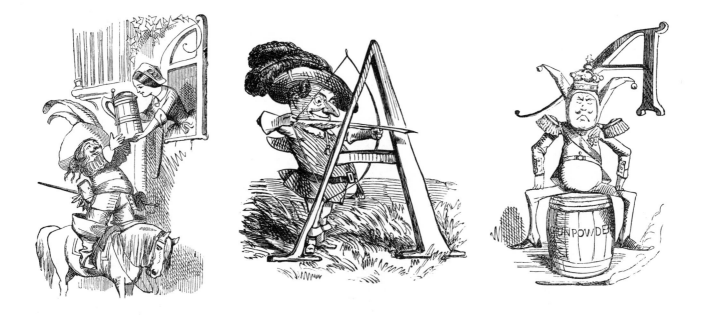

B

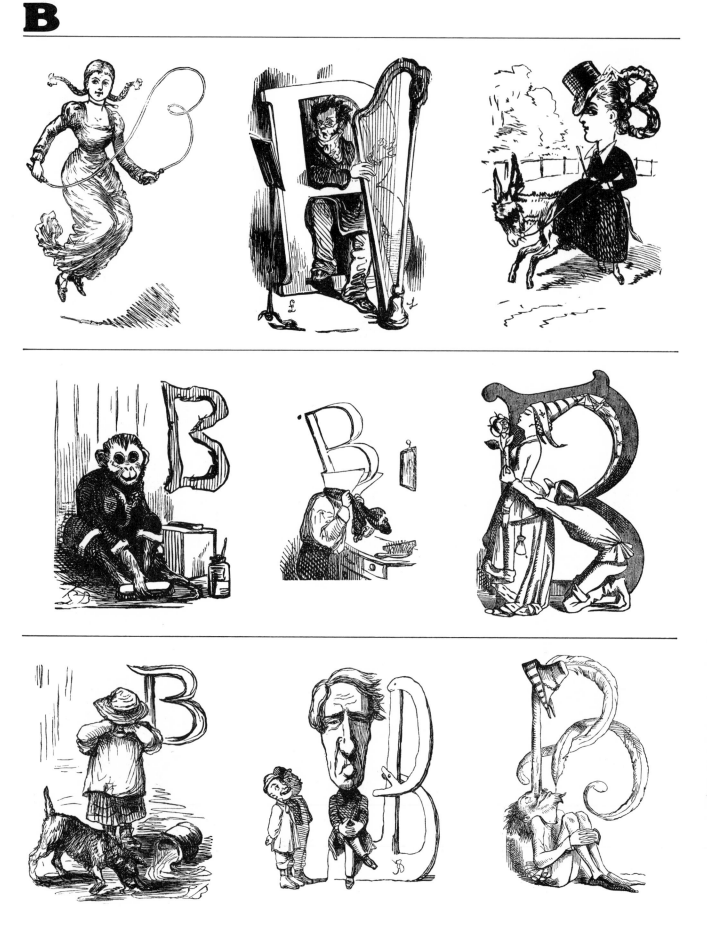

C

21

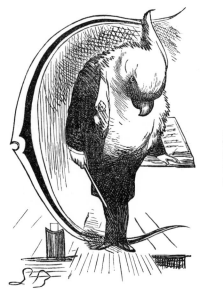  

D

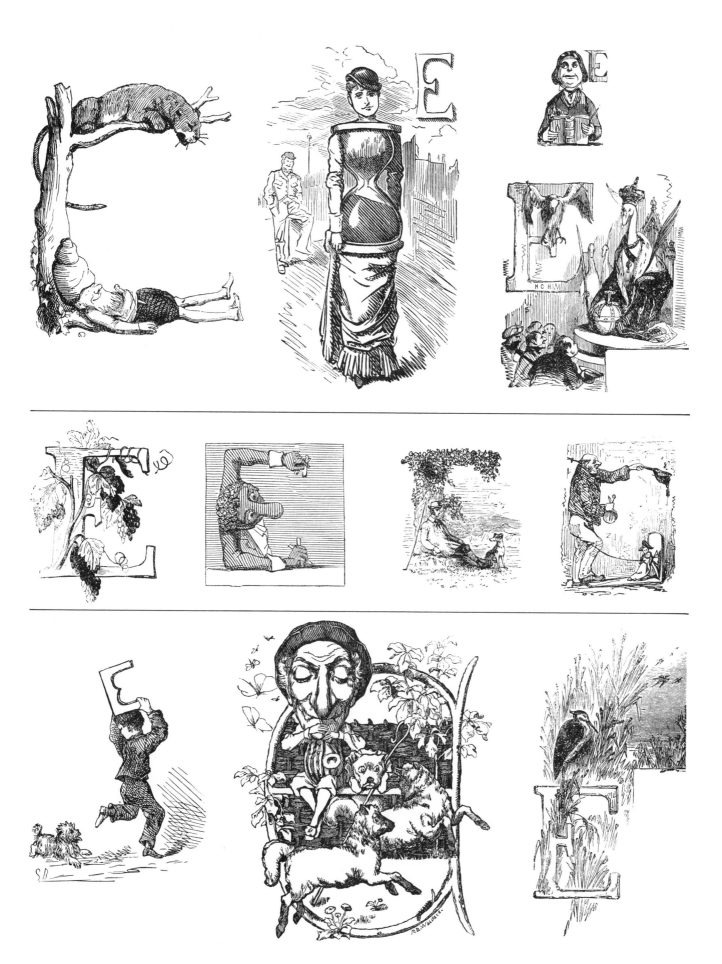

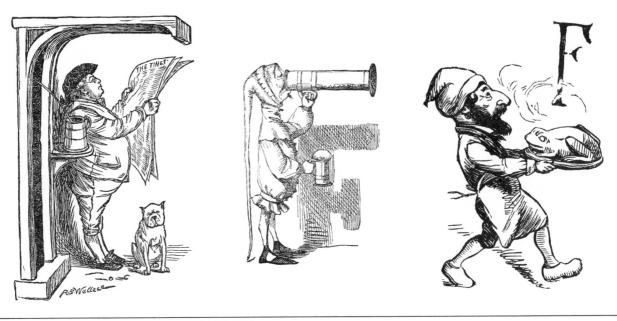

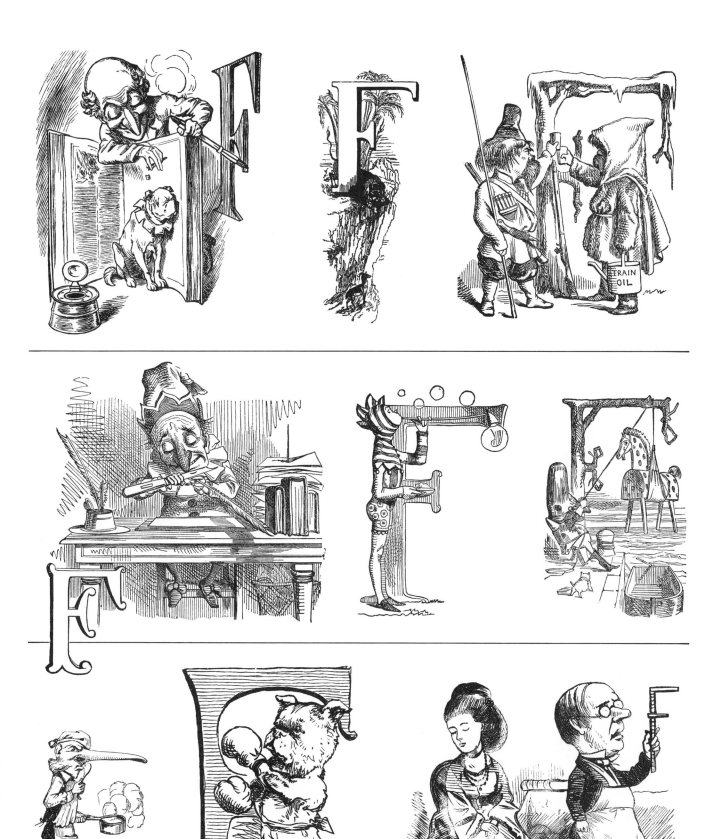

G

H

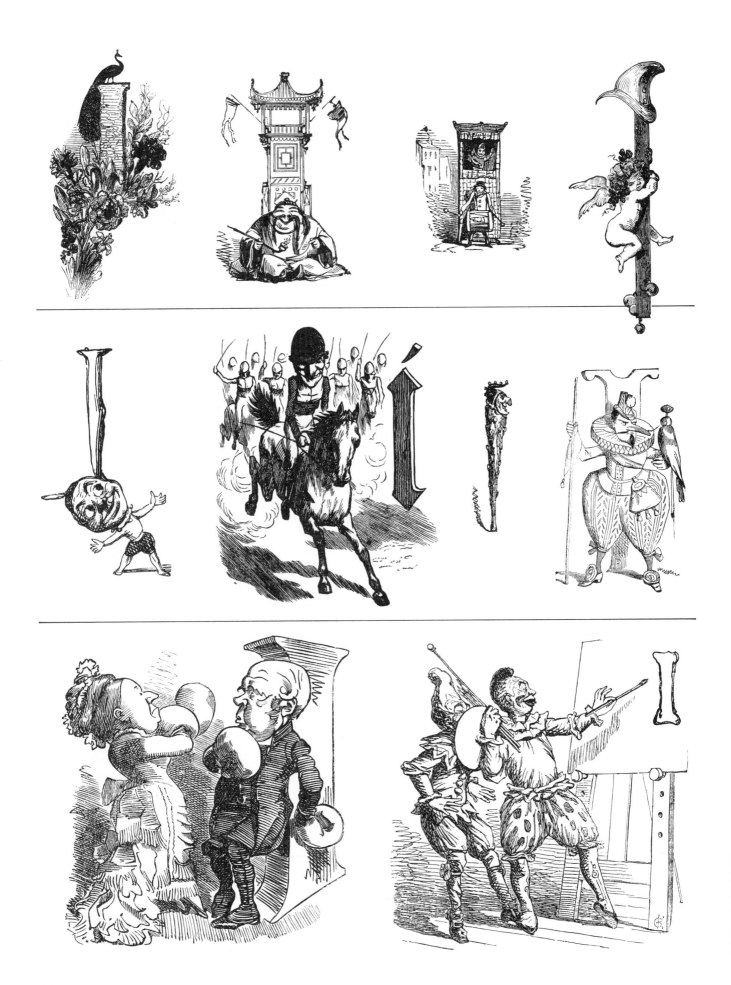

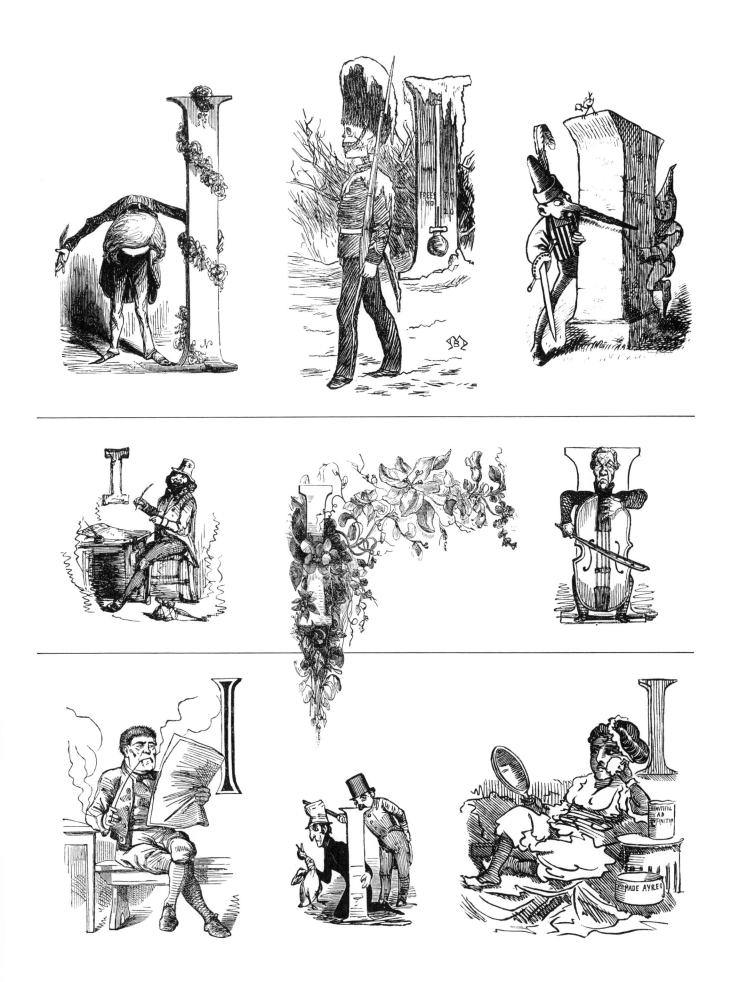

K

M

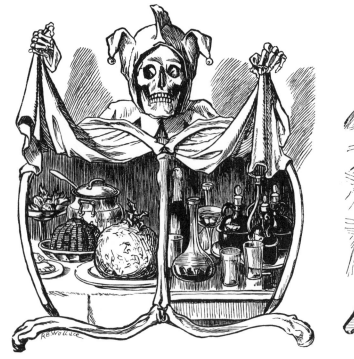

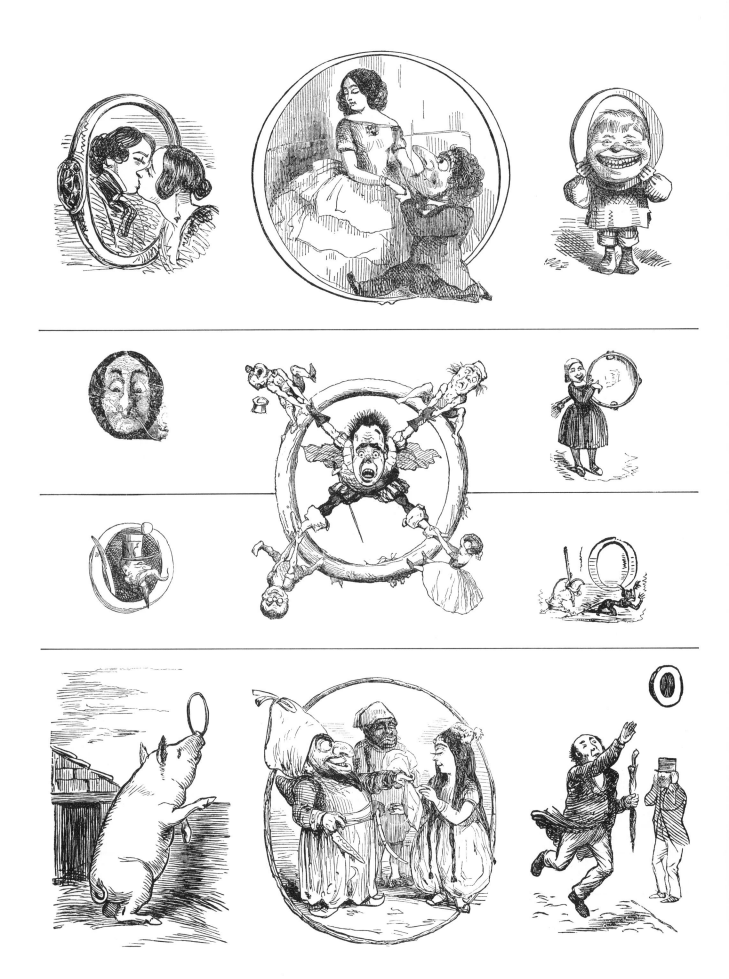

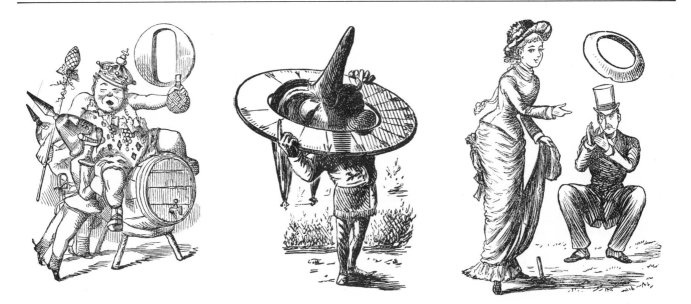

P

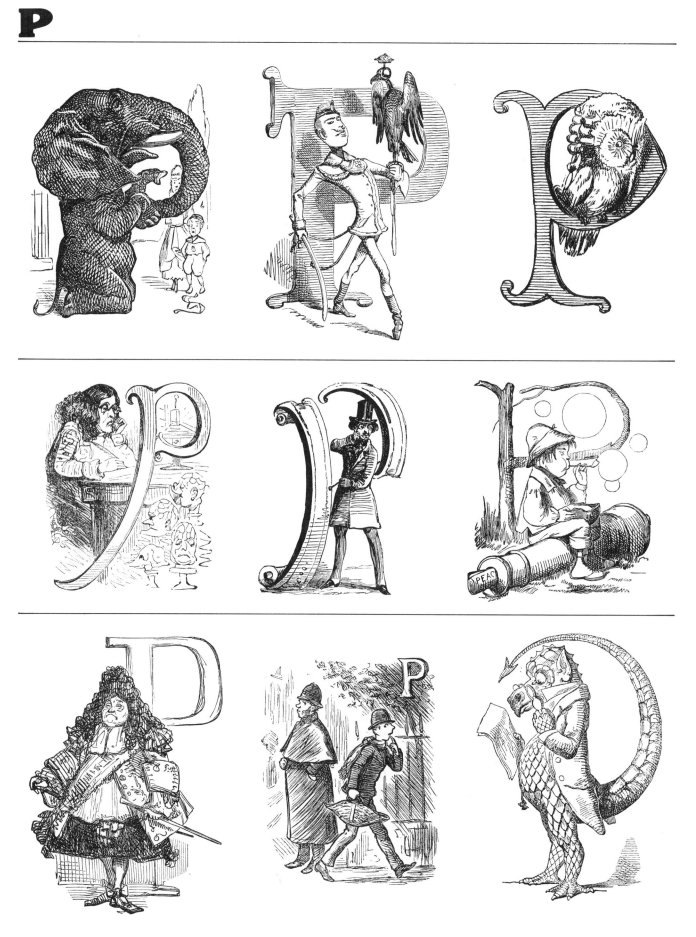

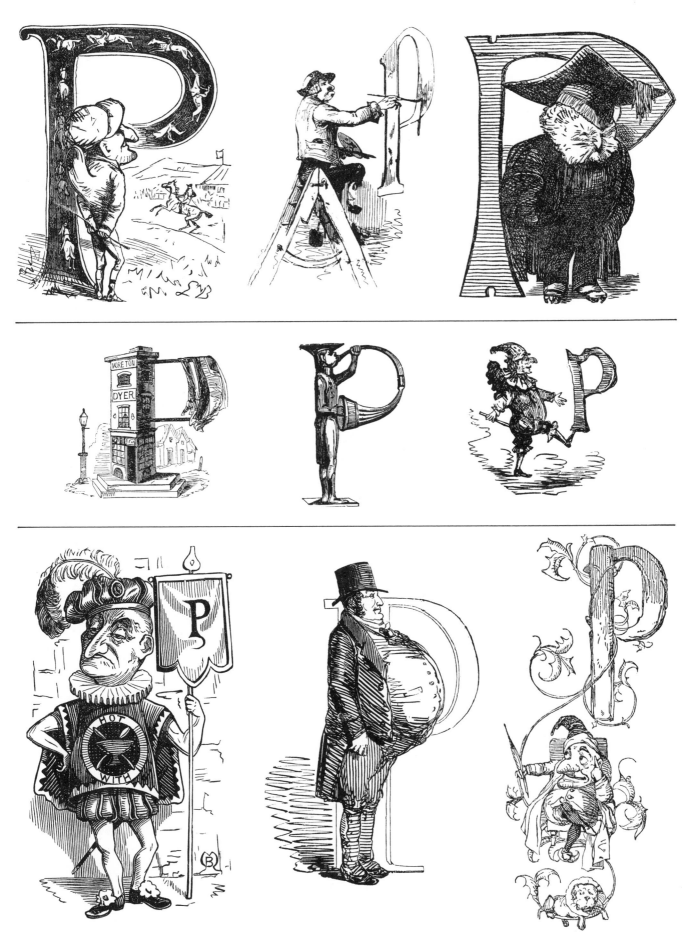

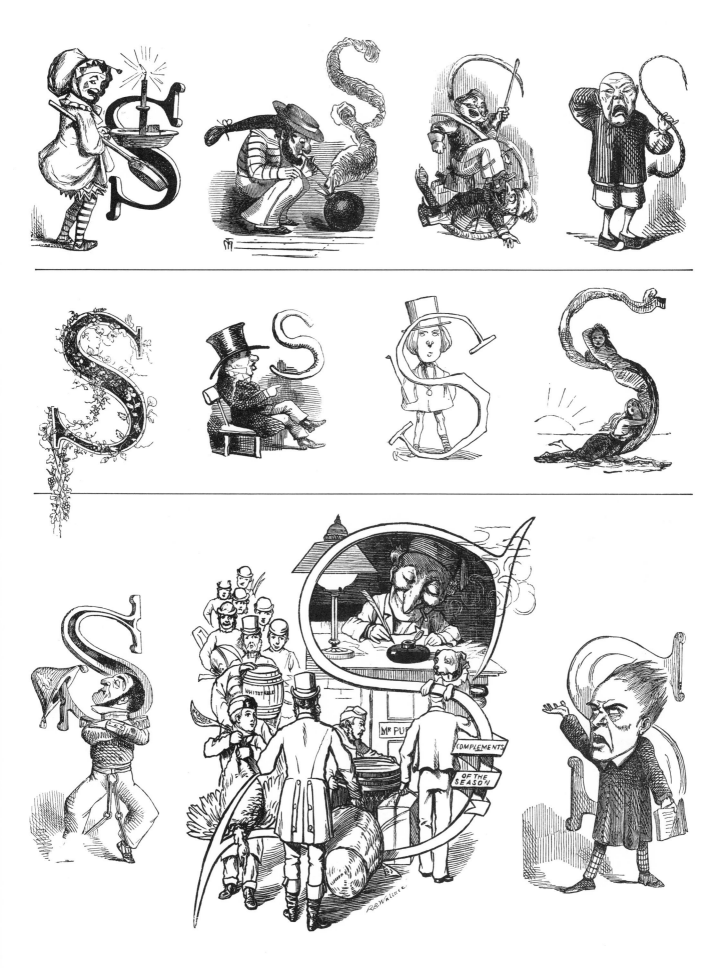

I am Starving

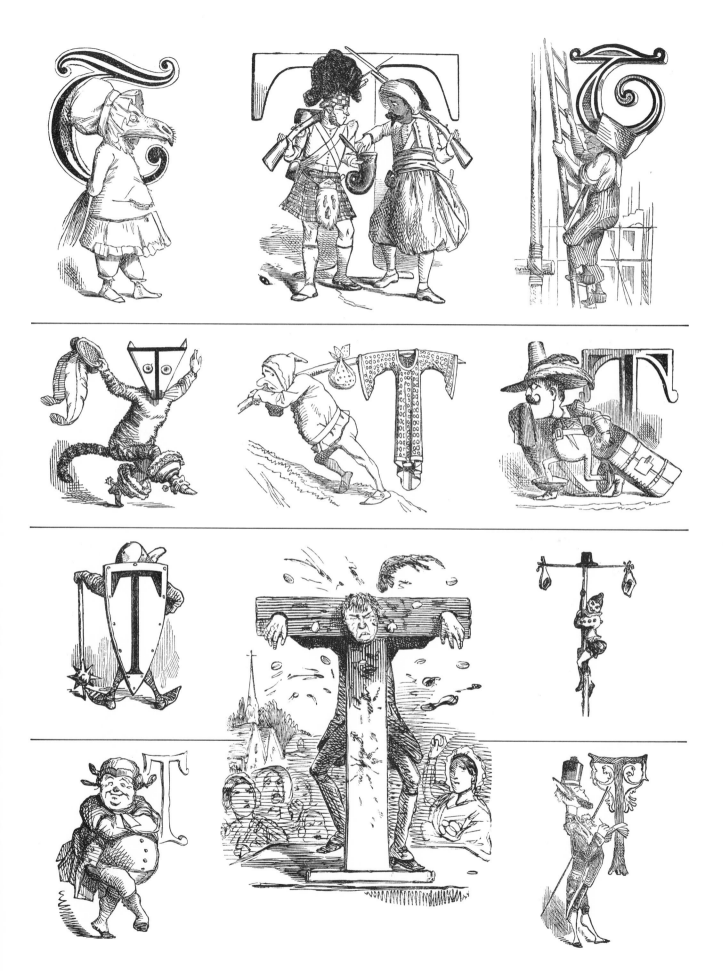

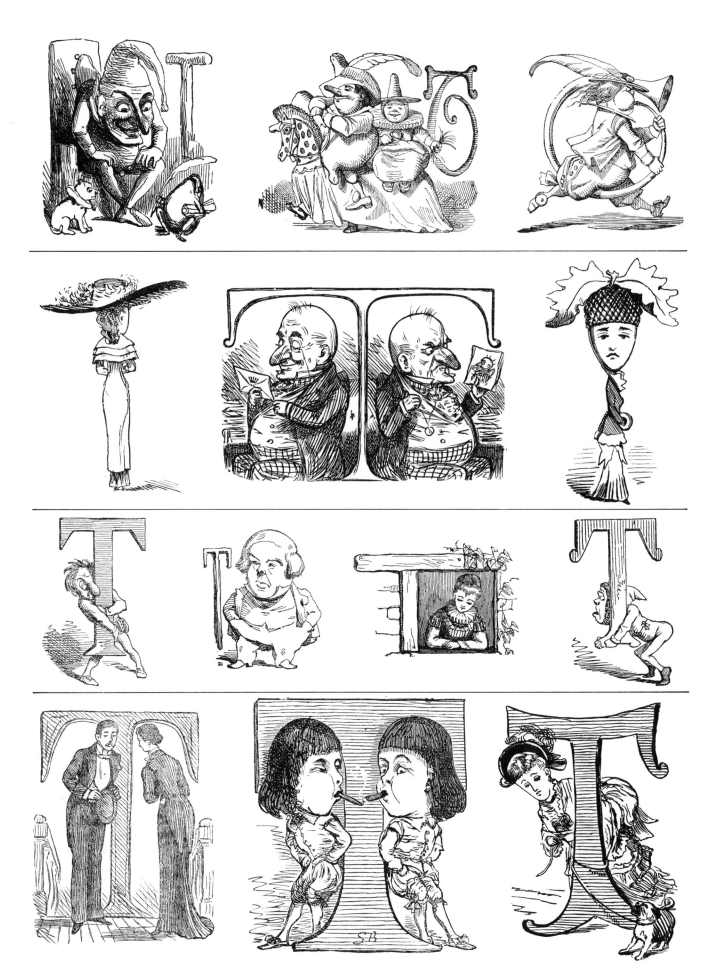

V

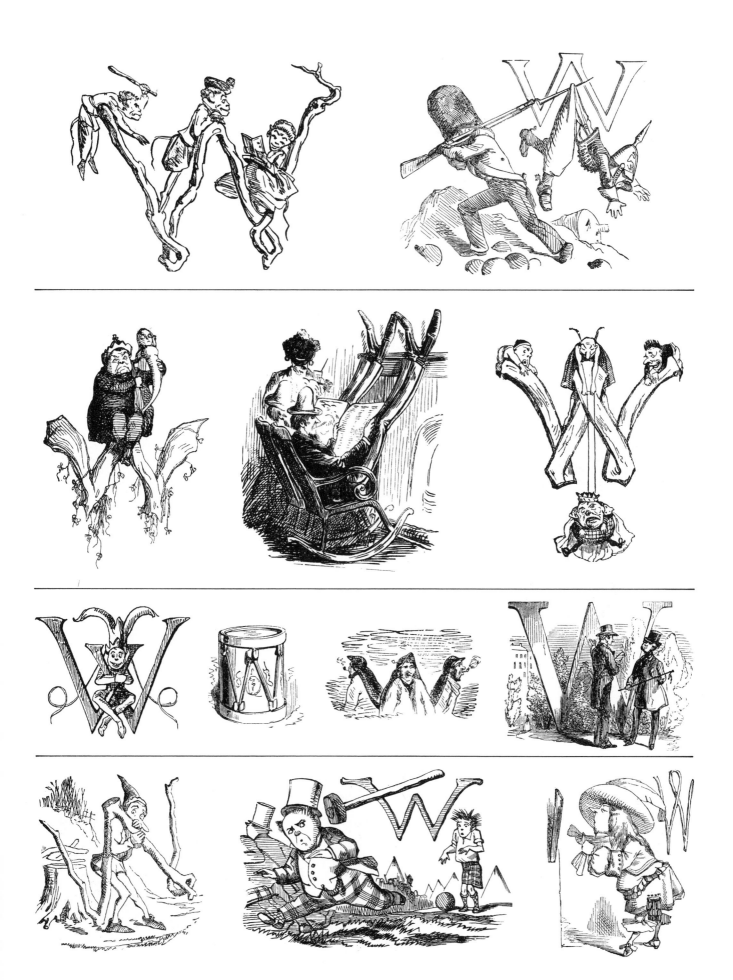

X

Y

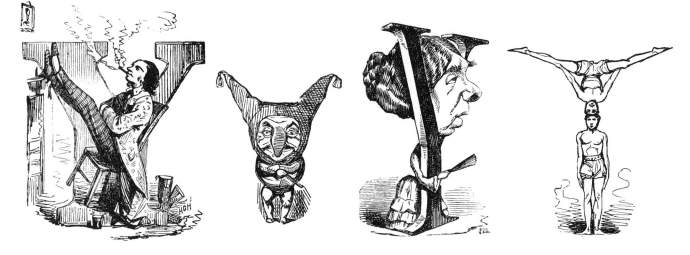

z

Miscellaneous

124